A Timeless Resource
for Congregation and Choir

D1567819

EVERLASTING
PRAISE

Arranged by

MIKE SPECK &
STAN WHITMIRE

Orchestrated by

WAYNE HAUN

PUBLISHING COMPANY

lillenas.com

TOP OF MY LUNGS

includes

Blessed Assurance
Top of My Lungs
O How I Love Jesus
I Love You, Lord

*Arr. by Mike Speck
and Stan Whitmire*

For medleys following the tracks, perform the endings marked with asterisks.

Blessed Assurance

FANNY J. CROSBY

PHOEBE PALMER KNAPP
*Arr. by Mike Speck
and Stan Whitmire*

CD 1:2

God,_____ Born of His Spir - it, washed in His blood!_____ This is my

sto - ry, this is my song,_____ Prais-ing my Sav - ior all the day

long._____ This is my sto - ry, this is my song,_____ Prais-ing my

CD 1:3

Song ending

*Medley ending

Sav - ior all the day long. long._____

Top of My Lungs

Words and Music by
TONY WOOD
*Arr. by Mike Speck
and Stan Whitmire*

O How I Love Jesus

FREDERICK WHITFIELD

Traditional American Melody
*Arr. by Mike Speck
and Stan Whitmire*

I Love You, Lord

Words and Music by
LAURIE KLEIN
*Arr. by Mike Speck
and Stan Whitmire*

CHRIST IS ALIVE

includes
Because He Lives
Alive Forever Amen
Christ Arose
He Is Lord

Arr. by Mike Speck
and Stan Whitmire

For medleys following the tracks, perform the endings marked with asterisks.

Because He Lives

GLORIA GAITHER and
WILLIAM J. GAITHER

WILLIAM J. GAITHER
Arr. by Mike Speck
and Stan Whitmire

12

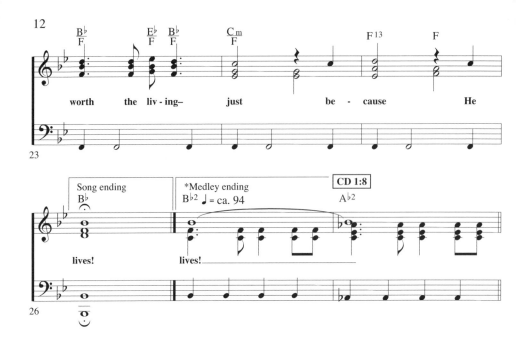

worth the liv-ing– just be - cause He

Song ending   *Medley ending   **CD 1:8**
lives!   lives!

Alive Forever Amen

Words and Music by
DAVID MOFFITT, SUE C. SMITH
and TRAVIS COTTRELL
*Arr. by Mike Speck
and Stan Whitmire*

He's a-live,_____ a-live,____ a-live

___ hal - le - lu - jah. A-live, praise and glo-ry to___ the Lamb.

Christ Arose

Words and Music by
ROBERT LOWRY
*Arr. by Mike Speck
and Stan Whitmire*

14

16

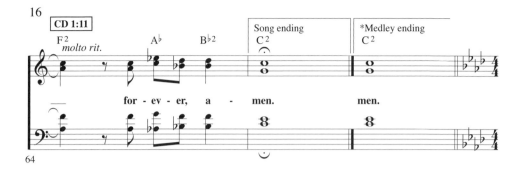

He Is Lord

Words and Music
Traditional
*Arr. by Mike Speck
and Stan Whitmire*

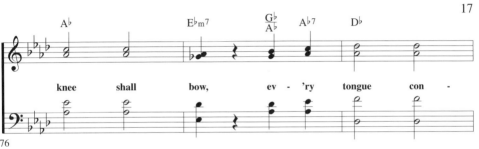

knee shall bow, ev - 'ry tongue con -

76

fess That Je - sus Christ is

79

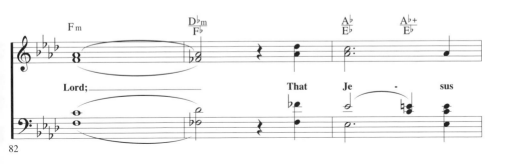

Lord; That Je - sus

82

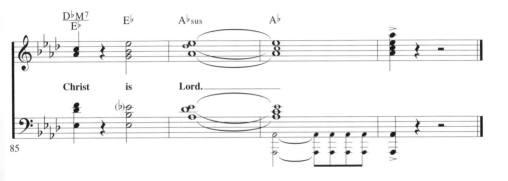

Christ is Lord.

85

WORSHIP JESUS
includes
Worship You, Jesus
You're Worthy of My Praise
Here I Am to Worship

*Arr. by Mike Speck
and Stan Whitmire*

For medleys following the tracks, perform the endings marked with asterisks.

Worship You, Jesus

Words and Music by
GERON DAVIS
*Arr. by Mike Speck
and Stan Whitmire*

19

20

CD 1:13

I give You all of the glo - ry

and I give You the praise.___ Lord, You are ho -

CD 1:14

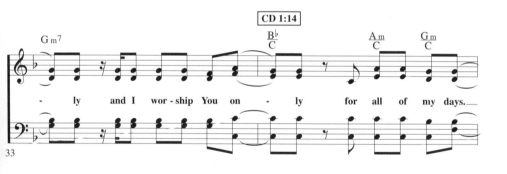

- ly and I wor - ship You on - ly for all of my days.___

Song ending

*Medley ending

You're Worthy of My Praise

Words and Music by
DAVID RUIS
Arr. by Mike Speck
and Stan Whitmire

24

CD 1:15

26

You a-lone___ I long to wor - ship.

You a-lone___ are wor - thy of___ my___

Song ending
F
praise.___

*Medley ending
F ♩ = ca. 67
praise.___

68

70

72

Here I Am to Worship

Words and Music by
TIM HUGHES
Arr. by Mike Speck
and Stan Whitmire

♩ = ca. 67

CD 1:16

Parts *mp*

mp

Here I am to

mp

74

IN CHRIST ALONE

includes

In Christ Alone
Lamb of God
Jesus Paid It All

Arr. by Mike Speck
and Stan Whitmire

For medleys following the tracks, perform the endings marked with asterisks.

In Christ Alone

Words and Music by
STUART TOWNEND
and KEITH GETTY
Arr. by Mike Speck
and Stan Whitmire

Medley Sequence copyright © 2008 by PsalmSinger Music (BMI). All rights reserved.
Administered by The Copyright Company, PO Box 128139, Nashville, TN 37212-8139.

PLEASE NOTE: Copying of this product is NOT covered by CCLI licenses. For CCLI information call 1-800-234-2446.

29

30

CD 1:18

32

grave He rose a - gain. And as He stands in vic - to -

ry, Sin's curse has lost its grip on me; For I am

Unison

CD 1:20

His and He is mine, bought with the

Song ending

pre - cious blood of Christ.

*Medley ending

Parts

pre - cious blood of Christ.

Lamb of God

Words and Music by
TWILA PARIS
Arr. by Mike Speck
and Stan Whitmire

♩ = ca. 67

Parts f

| Eb | Bb/D | Cm | Ab2 | Eb/G | Eb | Bb/D |

O Lamb of God, sweet Lamb of____ God; I love the

CD 1:21

| Cm | Ab2 | Bbsus | Bb | Cm | Eb/Bb | Ab |

ho — ly Lamb of____ God. O wash me in His pre - cious blood.____

68

Jesus Paid It All

ELVINA M. HALL

JOHN T. GRAPE
Arr. by Mike Speck
and Stan Whitmire

♩ = ca. 67

Eb
mp
Unison

| Ab/Eb | Eb/G | Cm7 |

Je - sus paid it all; All to Him I

72

34

THE LORD IS HOLY

includes
Holy Is the Lord
Shout to the Lord
How Great Thou Art
How Great Is Our God

Arr. by Mike Speck
and Stan Whitmire

For medleys following the tracks, perform the endings marked with asterisks.

Holy Is the Lord

Words and Music by
CHRIS TOMLIN
and LOUIE GIGLIO
Arr. by Mike Speck
and Stan Whitmire

Shout to the Lord

Words and Music by
DARLENE ZSCHECH
Arr. by Mike Speck
and Stan Whitmire

Shout to the Lord, all the earth let us sing

Pow- er and maj- es- ty, praise to the King.

Moun- tains bow down and the seas will roar at the

sound of Your name.

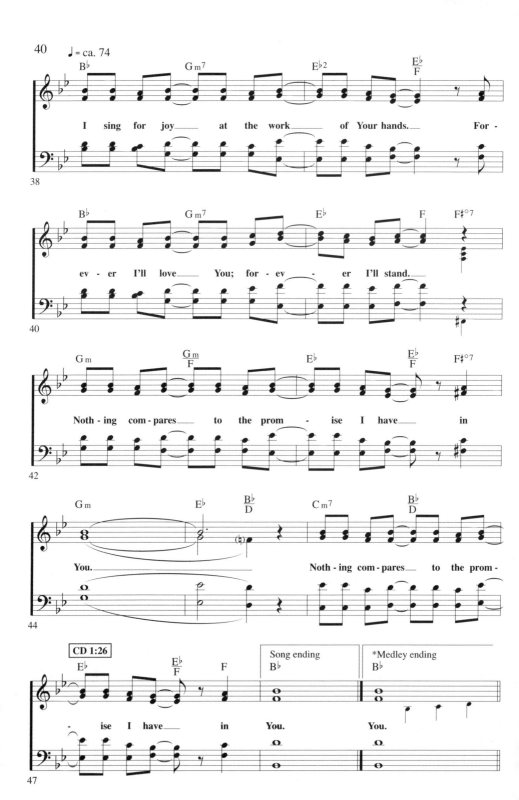

How Great Thou Art

Words and Music by
STUART K. HINE
*Arr. by Mike Speck
and Stan Whitmire*

42

How Great Is Our God

Words and Music by
CHRIS TOMLIN, ED CASH
and JESSE REEVES
*Arr. by Mike Speck
and Stan Whitmire*

Sing with me____ how great is our God.

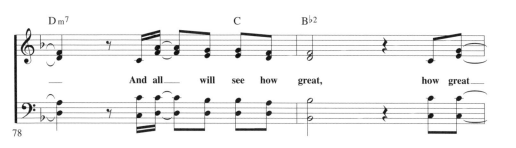

And all____ will see how great, how great____

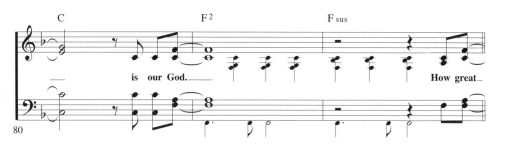

is our God.____ How great____

is our God.____ Sing with me____ how

great   is our God.   And all   will see how

85

great,   how great   is our God.

87

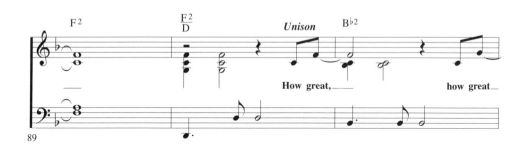

How great,   how great

89

is our God.

92

HAPPY MEDLEY

includes
He Keeps Me Singing
Since Jesus Came into My Heart
The Happy Song
He Has Made Me Glad

Arr. by Mike Speck
and Stan Whitmire

For medleys following the tracks, perform the endings marked with asterisks.

He Keeps Me Singing

Words and Music by
LUTHER B. BRIDGERS
Arr. by Mike Speck
and Stan Whitmire

Since Jesus Came into My Heart

RUFUS H. MCDANIEL

CHARLES H. GABRIEL
*Arr. by Mike Speck
and Stan Whitmire*

The Happy Song

Words and Music by
MARTIN SMITH
*Arr. by Mike Speck
and Stan Whitmire*

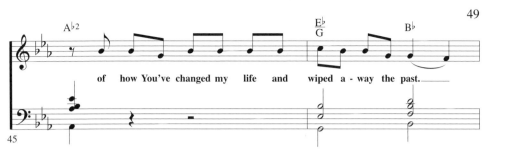

of how You've changed my life and wiped a - way the past.

I wan - na shout it out,___ from ev - 'ry roof - top sing,

for now I know that God is for me, not a - gainst me.

D.S. al Coda
(to pg. 48, meas. 35)

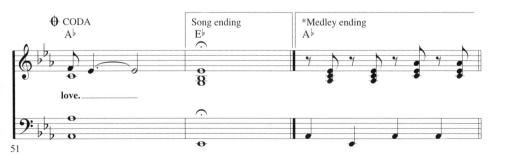

CODA
love.___

Song ending

*Medley ending

He Has Made Me Glad

Words and Music by
LEONA VON BRETHORST
Arr. by Mike Speck and Stan Whitmire

HE THOUGHT OF ME

includes
At the Cross
How Great Thou Art
Above All
When He Was on the Cross
The Old Rugged Cross

*Arr. by Mike Speck
and Stan Whitmire*

For medleys following the tracks, perform the endings marked with asterisks.

At the Cross

ISAAC WATTS

RALPH E. HUDSON
*Arr. by Mike Speck
and Stan Whitmire*

How Great Thou Art

Words and Music by
STUART K. HINE
Arr. by Mike Speck
and Stan Whitmire

Above All

Words and Music by
LENNY LEBLANC
and PAUL BALOCHE
*Arr. by Mike Speck
and Stan Whitmire*

(to pg. 55, meas. 32)

When He Was on the Cross

Words and Music by
MIKE PAYNE and
RONNY HINSON
*Arr. by Mike Speck
and Stan Whitmire*

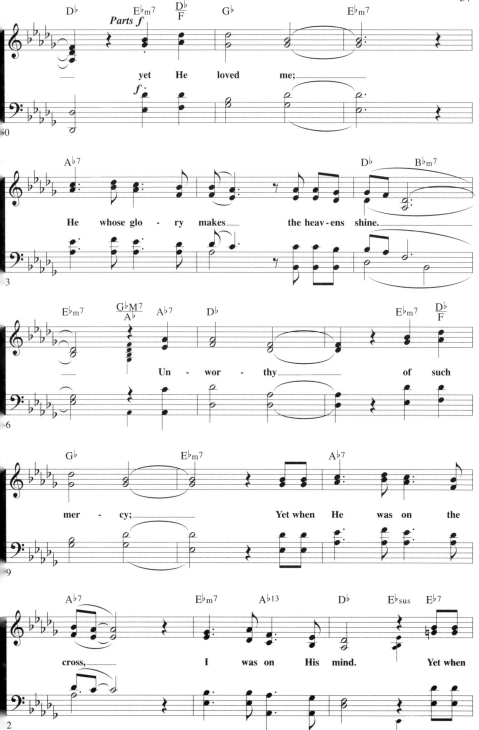

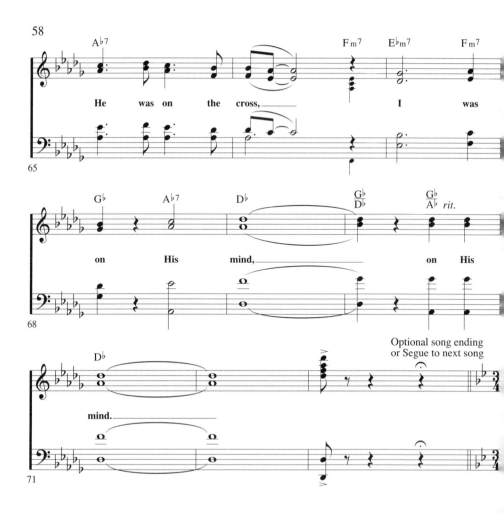

Optional song ending
or Segue to next song

The Old Rugged Cross

Words and Music by
GEORGE BENNARD
*Arr. by Mike Speck
and Stan Whitmire*

JESUS' NAME

includes
The Name of the Lord
Blessed Be Your Name
Blessed Be the Name
Your Name

*Arr. by Mike Speck
and Stan Whitmire*

For medleys following the tracks, perform the endings marked with asterisks.

The Name of the Lord

Words and Music by
CLINTON HUBERT UTTERBACH
*Arr. by Mike Speck
and Stan Whitmire*

61

64

Bless - ed be the name of the Lord;

Bless - ed be the name of the Lord_____ Most_____ High.

CD 1:43

Song ending

*Medley ending

Blessed Be Your Name

Words and Music by
MATT REDMAN and
BETH REDMAN
*Arr. by Mike Speck
and Stan Whitmire*

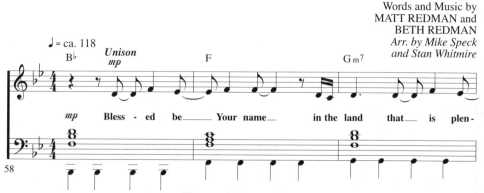

♩ = ca. 118
Unison
mp

Bless - ed be_____ Your name_____ in the land that_____ is plen-

65

66

CD 1:44

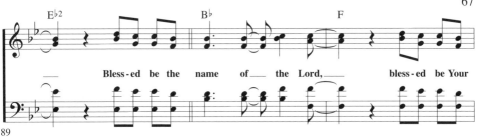

Bless-ed be the name of ___ the Lord, ___ bless-ed be Your

89

name. ___ Bless-ed be the name of ___ the Lord, ___

92

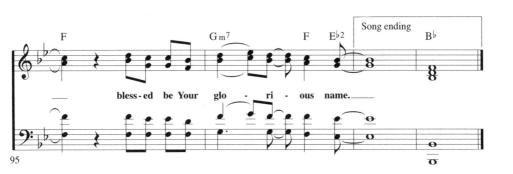

___ bless-ed be Your glo - ri - ous name. ___

Song ending

95

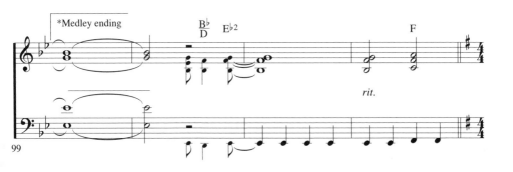

*Medley ending

rit.

99

Blessed Be the Name

CHARLES WESLEY
Refrain RALPH E. HUDSON

Anonymous
*Arr. by Mike Speck
and Stan Whitmire*

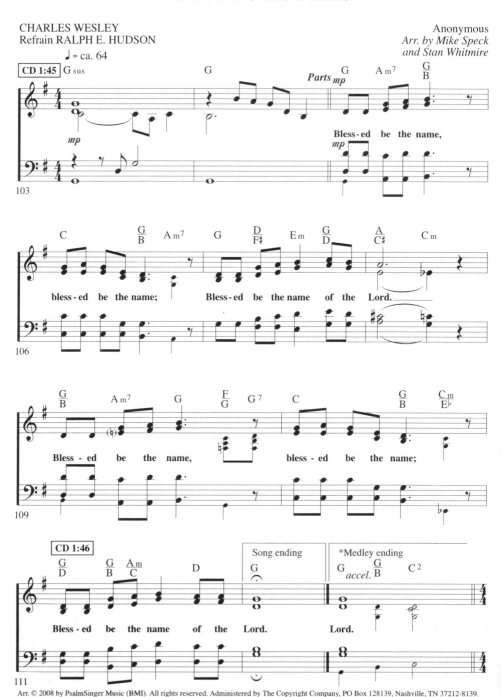

Your Name

Words and Music by
PAUL BALOCHE and
GLENN PACKIAM
*Arr. by Mike Speck
and Stan Whitmire*

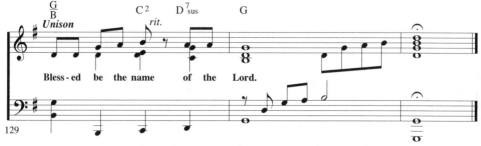

SALVATION MEDLEY

includes
Jesus Saves!
Mighty to Save

*Arr. by Mike Speck
and Stan Whitmire*

For medleys following the tracks, perform the endings marked with asterisks.

Jesus Saves!

PRISCILLA J. OWENS

WILLIAM J. KIRKPATRICK
*Arr. by Mike Speck
and Stan Whitmire*

72

76

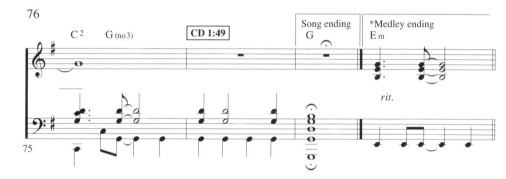

Mighty to Save

Words and Music by
BEN FIELDING and
REUBEN MORGAN
*Arr. by Mike Speck
and Stan Whitmire*

SING TO THE KING MEDLEY

includes
O Worship the King
Sing to the King
You Are My King

Arr. by Mike Speck
and Stan Whitmire

For medleys following the tracks, perform the endings marked with asterisks.

O Worship the King

ROBERT GRANT

Attr. to
JOHANN MICHAEL HAYDN
Arr. by Mike Speck
and Stan Whitmire

80

Sing to the King

Words and Music by
BILLY FOOTE and
CHARLES SILVESTER HORNE
*Arr. by Mike Speck
and Stan Whitmire*

Sing to the King Who is com - ing to reign;

Glo - ry to Je - sus, the

Lamb that was slain. Life and sal -

va - tion His em - pire shall bring;

82

CD 1:54

Joy to___ the na - tions when Je - sus___ is

King.___ Come let us sing___

a song, a song de-clar - ing we___ be - long___ to Je -

- sus;___ He's all___ we___ need.

Lift up a heart___ of praise;___

2nd time to Coda (to pg. 84, meas. 79)

Sing now with voic - es raised_ to Je - sus;_

CD 1:55

Sing to_ the_ King._

For His_ re -

turn - ing_ we watch and_ we pray;_

We will_ be read - y the dawn of_ that

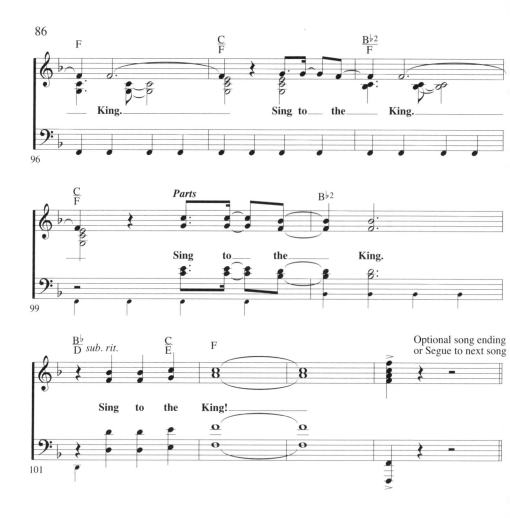

You Are My King

Words and Music by
BRIAN DOERKSEN
*Arr. by Mike Speck
and Stan Whitmire*

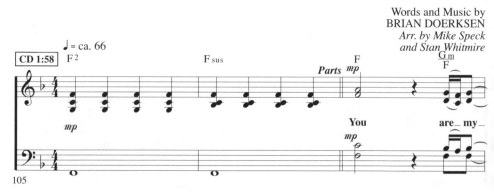

88

Amazing Grace
(My Chains Are Gone)

Words and Music by
CHRIS TOMLIN
and LOUIE GIGLIO
*Arr. by Mike Speck
and Stan Whitmire*

90

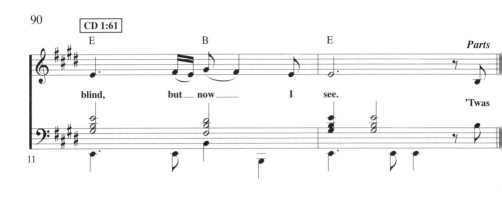

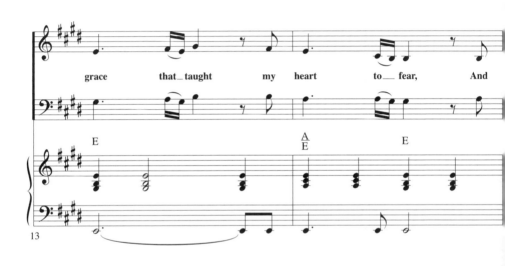

CD 1:62

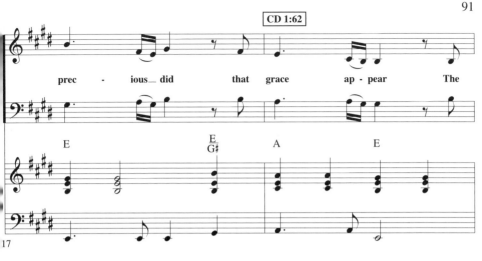

prec - ious__ did that grace ap - pear The

hour I__ first____ be - lieved! My chains are

gone, I've been set____ free; My God, my

92

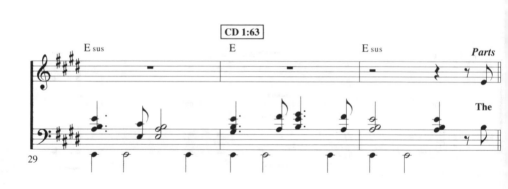

94

96

97

LET IT RISE

includes
Holy, Holy, Holy
Let It Rise
Let There Be Glory and Honor and Praises

Arr. by Mike Speck
and Stan Whitmire

For medleys following the tracks, perform the endings marked with asterisks.

Holy, Holy, Holy

Words and Music by
GARY OLIVER
Arr. by Mike Speck
and Stan Whitmire

Let It Rise

Words and Music by
HOLLAND DAVIS
*Arr. by Mike Speck
and Stan Whitmire*

102

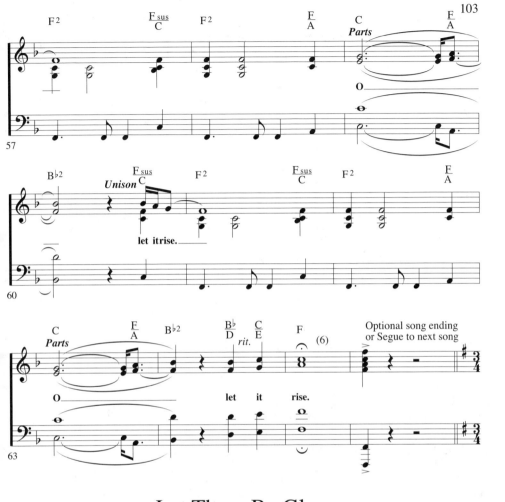

Let There Be Glory
and Honor and Praises

Words and Music by
ELIZABETH GREENELSH
*Arr. by Mike Speck
and Stan Whitmire*

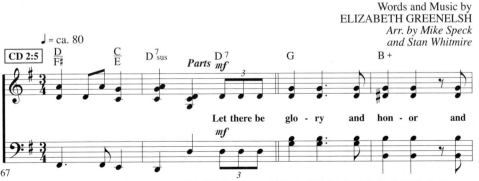

SERVE THE LORD

includes
What a Mighty God We Serve
Love the Lord
Evermore

*Arr. by Mike Speck
and Stan Whitmire*

For medleys following the tracks, perform the endings marked with asterisks.

What a Mighty God We Serve

Words and Music
Anonymous
*Arr. by Mike Speck
and Stan Whitmire*

106

Love the Lord

Words and Music by
LINCOLN BREWSTER
*Arr. by Mike Speck
and Stan Whitmire*

108

CD 2:9

and with all my strength.

I will serve the Lord with all my heart, with all my soul, with all my

CD 2:10

Unison

Song ending

*Medley ending

mind, and with all my strength. strength.

Evermore

Words and Music by
GERON DAVIS
*Arr. by Mike Speck
and Stan Whitmire*

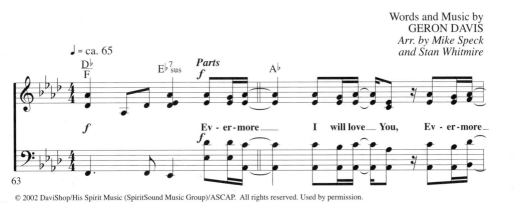

♩ = ca. 65

Parts

Ev-er-more I will love You, Ev-er-more

112

STAND FOR JESUS

includes
Stand Up, Stand Up for Jesus
Victory in Jesus

Arr. by Mike Speck
and Stan Whitmire

For medleys following the tracks, perform the endings marked with asterisks.

Stand Up, Stand Up for Jesus

GEORGE DUFFIELD

GEORGE J. WEBB
Arr. by Mike Speck
and Stan Whitmire

115

Victory in Jesus

Words and Music by
EUGENE M. BARTLETT
*Arr. by Mike Speck
and Stan Whitmire*

118

MY REDEEMER LIVES

includes

Christ the Lord Is Risen Today
My Redeemer Lives
Redeemer
He Lives

Arr. by Mike Speck
and Stan Whitmire

For medleys following the tracks, perform the endings marked with asterisks.

Christ the Lord Is Risen Today

CHARLES WESLEY

Lyra Davidica, 1708
Arr. by Mike Speck
and Stan Whitmire

120

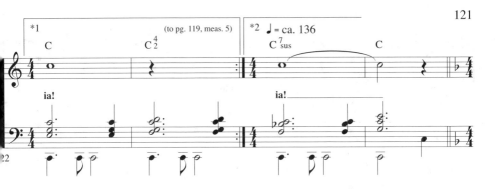

My Redeemer Lives

Words and Music by
REUBEN MORGAN
*Arr. by Mike Speck
and Stan Whitmire*

124

Redeemer

He Lives

Words and Music by
ALFRED H. ACKLEY
*Arr. by Mike Speck
and Stan Whitmire*

126

WORTHY IS THE LAMB

includes
Thank You, Lord
Worthy Is the Lamb
We Fall Down
I Will Praise Him

*Arr. by Mike Speck
and Stan Whitmire*

For medleys following the tracks, perform the endings marked with asterisks.

Thank You, Lord

Words and Music by
SETH and BESSIE SYKES
*Arr. by Mike Speck
and Stan Whitmire*

Medley Sequence copyright © 2008 by PsalmSinger Music (BMI). All rights reserved.
Administered by The Copyright Company, PO Box 128139, Nashville, TN 37212-8139.

PLEASE NOTE: Copying of this product is NOT covered by CCLI licenses. For CCLI information call 1-800-234-2446.

Worthy Is the Lamb

Words and Music by
DARLENE ZSCHECH
Arr. by Mike Speck
and Stan Whitmire

130

We Fall Down

Words and Music by
CHRIS TOMLIN
*Arr. by Mike Speck
and Stan Whitmire*

I Will Praise Him

Words and Music by
MARGARET J. HARRIS
Arr. by Mike Speck
and Stan Whitmire

THE VICTOR'S SONG

includes
We've Come This Far by Faith
We're Marching to Zion
Press On

*Arr. by Mike Speck
and Stan Whitmire*

For medleys following the tracks, perform the endings marked with asterisks.

We've Come This Far by Faith

Words and Music by
ALBERT GOODSON
*Arr. by Mike Speck
and Stan Whitmire*

Medley Sequence copyright © 2008 by PsalmSinger Music (BMI). All rights reserved.
Administered by The Copyright Company, PO Box 128139, Nashville, TN 37212-8139.

PLEASE NOTE: Copying of this product is NOT covered by CCLI licenses. For CCLI information call 1-800-234-2446.

136

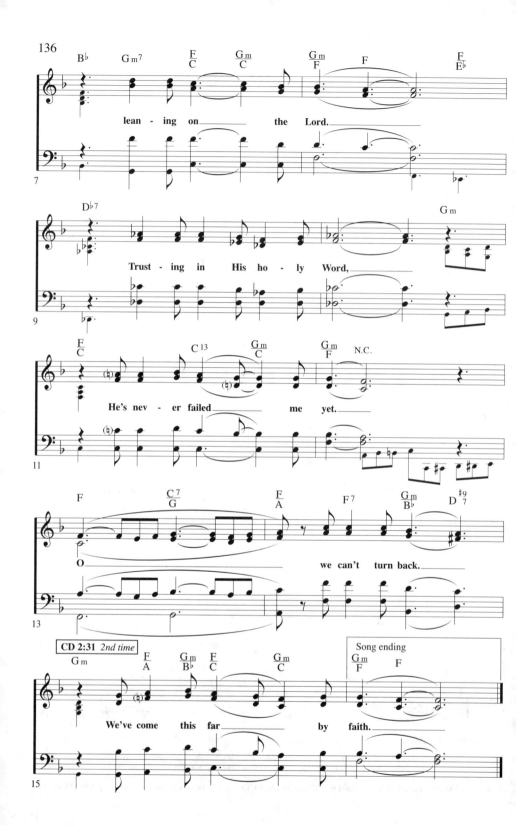

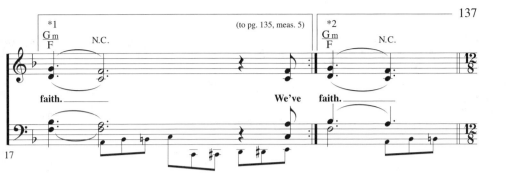

We're Marching to Zion

Words and Music by
ROBERT LOWRY
*Arr. by Mike Speck
and Stan Whitmire*

138

beau - ti - ful cit - y ___ of God.   We've

come this far ___ by faith, ___   lean - ing on ___ the

Lord. ___   Trust - ing in His ho - ly

Word, ___   He's nev - er failed ___ me

yet. ___   O

Press On

Words and Music by
DAN BURGESS
*Arr. by Mike Speck
and Stan Whitmire*

HIS PRESENCE

includes
I Feel Jesus
O the Glory of Your Presence
Holy Spirit, Rain Down

*Arr. by Mike Speck
and Stan Whitmire*

For medleys following the tracks, perform the endings marked with asterisks.

I Feel Jesus

Words and Music by
CARMEN D. LICCIARDELLO
*Arr. by Mike Speck
and Stan Whitmire*

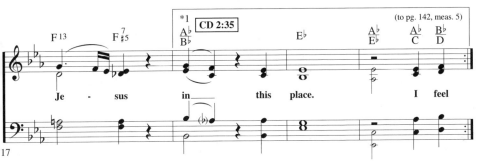

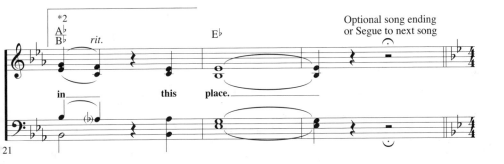

O the Glory of Your Presence

Words and Music by
STEVE FRY
*Arr. by Mike Speck
and Stan Whitmire*

brace;_____ As Your pres - ence now fills this

place. So a - rise to Your rest and be

blessed by our praise As we glo - ry in Your em -

brace;_____ As Your pres - ence now fills this

place. Fills this place._____

Optional song ending
or Segue to next song

Holy Spirit, Rain Down

Words and Music by
RUSSELL FRAGAR
*Arr. by Mike Speck
and Stan Whitmire*

148

GOD'S LOVE

includes
No Greater Love
Hallelujah (Your Love Is Amazing)
Forever

Arr. by Mike Speck
and Stan Whitmire

For medleys following the tracks, perform the endings marked with asterisks.

No Greater Love

Words and Music by
TOMMY WALKER
Arr. by Mike Speck
and Stan Whitmire

Medley Sequence copyright © 2008 by PsalmSinger Music (BMI). All rights reserved.
Administered by The Copyright Company, PO Box 128139, Nashville, TN 37212-8139.

PLEASE NOTE: Copying of this product is NOT covered by CCLI licenses. For CCLI information call 1-800-234-2446.

Hallelujah (Your Love Is Amazing)

Words and Music by
BRENTON BROWN and
BRIAN DOERKSEN
*Arr. by Mike Speck
and Stan Whitmire*

Forever

Words and Music by
CHRIS TOMLIN
*Arr. by Mike Speck
and Stan Whitmire*

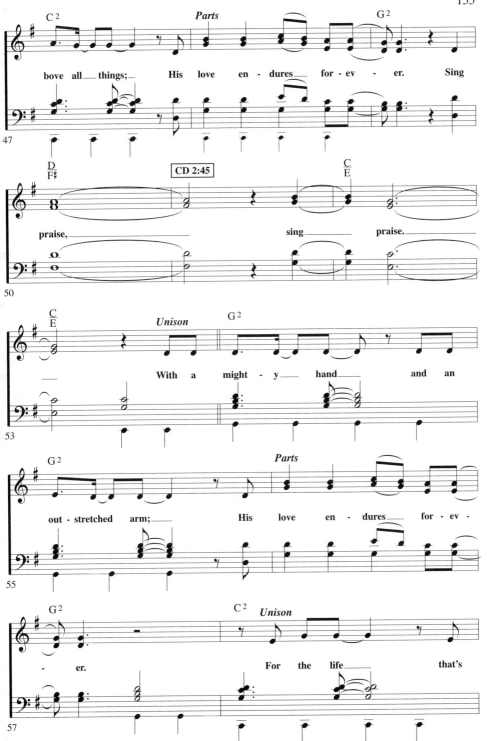

156

SWEETER MEDLEY

includes
Saved, Saved!
Sweeter
Sweeter As the Days Go By
The Longer I Serve Him

Arr. by Mike Speck
and Stan Whitmire

For medleys following the tracks, perform the endings marked with asterisks.

Saved, Saved!

Words and Music by
JACK P. SCHOLFIELD
Arr. by Mike Speck
and Stan Whitmire

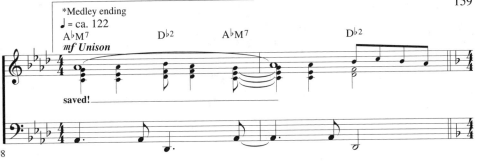

Sweeter

Words and Music by
CINDY CRUSE-RATCLIFF,
ISRAEL HOUGHTON and
MELEASA HOUGHTON
*Arr. by Mike Speck
and Stan Whitmire*

160

Sweeter As the Days Go By

Words and Music by
GENESER SMITH
*Arr. by Mike Speck
and Stan Whitmire*

162

The Longer I Serve Him

Words and Music by
WILLIAM J. GAITHER
*Arr. by Mike Speck
and Stan Whitmire*

The long - er I serve Him, the sweet - er He grows. The more that I love Him, more love He be - stows. Each

Untitled Hymn
(Come to Jesus)

Words and Music by
CHRIS RICE
Arr. by Mike Speck
and Stan Whitmire

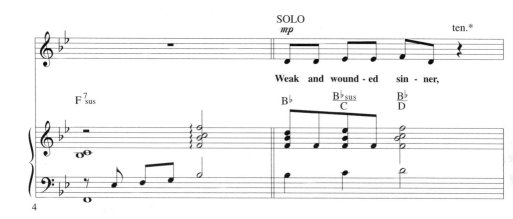

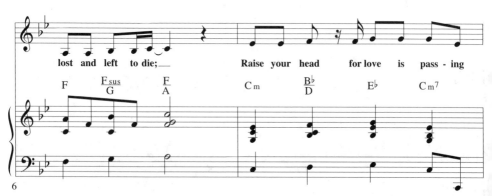

*Many measures in this arrangement should have a "tentative" marking on the 4th beat of the measure. Observe all when using track.

PLEASE NOTE: Copying of this product is NOT covered by CCLI licenses. For CCLI information call 1-800-234-2446.

SOLO *and* CHOIR

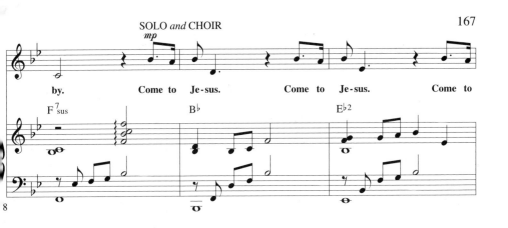

by.   Come to Je-sus.   Come to Je-sus.   Come to

Je - sus   and live.   Now your bur-den's lift-ed   and

car - ried far a-way___   And pre-cious blood   has washed a-way___

the stain.   So sing to Je-sus.   Sing to Je-sus.   Sing to

F⁷sus   F⁷   CHOIR   B♭   E♭2

Sing to Je-sus.   Sing to Je-sus.   Sing to

16

CD 2:56

mf

Je - sus and live.   Like a new-born ba-by,

B♭/F   F⁷sus F⁷   B♭   B   B sus/C♯   B/D♯

Je - sus and live.

19

don't be a-fraid to crawl.   And re-mem - ber   when you walk, some-times

F♯/G♯   F♯sus/G♯   F♯/A♯   C♯m   B/D♯   E   C♯m

22

170

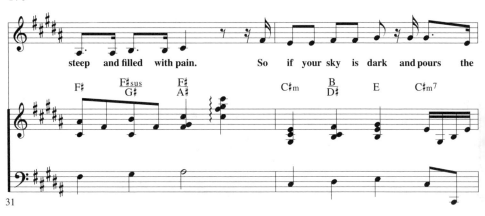

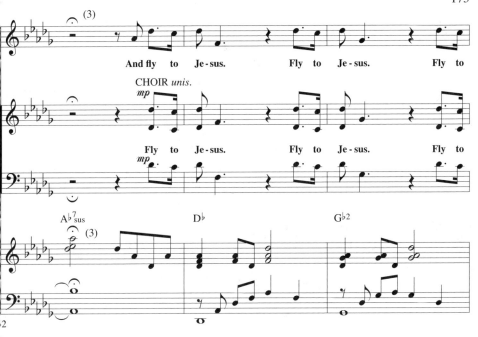

And fly to Je-sus. Fly to Je-sus. Fly to

CHOIR *unis.*

Fly to Je-sus. Fly to Je-sus. Fly to

A♭⁷sus   D♭   G♭2

CD 2:60

Je - sus and live.   Fly to

CHOIR *parts*

Je - sus and live.   Fly to

D♭/A♭   A♭⁷sus A♭/G♭   D♭/F   G♭2 G♭   D♭/A♭   A♭⁷sus A♭7

Je - sus.   Fly   to   Je - sus.   Fly   to

Je - sus.   Fly   to   Je - sus.   Fly   to

Db   Gb2

58

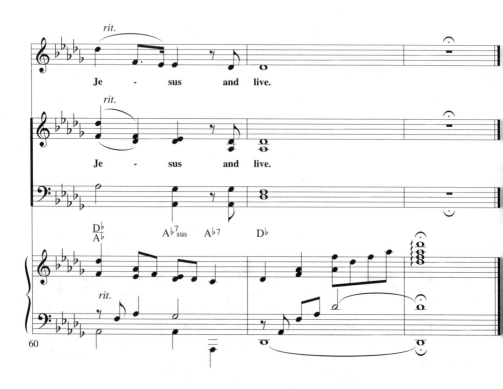

rit.

Je - sus   and   live.

rit.

Je - sus   and   live.

Db/Ab   Ab7sus   Ab7   Db

rit.

60

Topical Index of Medleys

Medley Index

Alphabetical Index
Song and MEDLEY Titles